PEOPLE OF WALMART.COM
OF THE PEOPLE, BY THE PEOPLE, FOR THE PEOPLE

Adam Kipple Andrew Kipple Luke Wherry

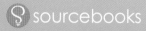

sourcebooks

Copyright © 2012 by Andrew Kipple, Adam Kipple, Luke Wherry
Cover and internal design © 2012 by Sourcebooks, Inc.
Cover design by William Riley/Sourcebooks
Cover images © Rafael Angel Irusta Machin/Dreamstime.com, © Pablo631/Dreamstime.com, © Chiyacat/Dreamstime.com, © Warren0909/
Dreamstime.com

Sourcebooks and the colophon are registered trademarks of Sourcebooks, Inc.

This publication is designed to provide accurate and authoritative information in regard to the subject matter covered. It is sold with the understanding
that the publisher is not engaged in rendering legal, accounting, or other professional service. If legal advice or other expert assistance is required, the
services of a competent professional person should be sought.–*From a Declaration of Principles Jointly Adopted by a Committee of the American Bar
Association and a Committee of Publishers and Associations*

All brand names and product names used in this book are trademarks, registered trademarks, or trade names of their respective holders. Sourcebooks,
Inc., is not associated with any product or vendor in this book.

Published by Sourcebooks, Inc.
P.O. Box 4410, Naperville, Illinois 60567-4410
(630) 961-3900
Fax: (630) 961-2168
www.sourcebooks.com

Library of Congress Cataloging-in-Publication Data

Kipple, Andrew.
  People of Walmart : of the people, by the people, for the people / Andrew Kipple, Adam Kipple, and Luke Wherry.
    p. cm.
  1. Shopping--United States–Humor. 2. Wal-Mart (Firm)–Humor. 3. American wit and humor, Pictorial. 4. United States–Civilization–21st century–
Humor. I. Kipple, Adam. II. Wherry, Luke. III. Title.
  PN6231.S5467K575 2012
  818'.60208–dc23

                                 2012012050

                          Printed and bound in China.
                          LEO 10 9 8 7 6 5 4 3 2 1

ACKNOWLEDGMENTS

First and foremost, we'd like to thank our friends and family for their support; we are honestly not sure how they do it, but they must be some pretty patient and loving people to put up with our dumb-asses. Our parents, Al and Elena Kipple and Tom and Diana Wherry, as well as Clint Wherry, have been doing it for twenty-some years now which is amazing, but then again it's their job, so we don't want them to get too excited about it, because they pretty much have to put up with us. However, Adam's wife, Bree, and Luke's wife, Mindy, both volunteered for this shit, so thank you both for lowering your standards for us!

We can't list all of our friends who have supported us on here, but we would like to point out some people we left out of our last book: Chris Matechen, Matt Montgomery, Ryan Archer, Nick Belleman, Trey "Trap" Borland, all my Xavier ladies and Valpo law school friends. Also, Brian Bausch, I spelled your name correctly this time, although I still contend it was our editor's fault. Lastly, I'd like to thank our entire Three Ring Blogs family: Debbie Suftko, Tim Brown, Sean Dillon, Jonny Shea, Jerad Friedline, Chris Arreguin, Bryan Yong, Danielle Knight, Mike Butler, George Bashaw, and Joan Conklin. Without you guys we wouldn't have the best jobs in the world.

Special thanks again to Brett Fullmer for keeping our website functional for the world to enjoy. Thank you to our literary agent Alison Fargis of Stonesong, as well as Peter Lynch and Anne Hartman of Sourcebooks, our fantastic publisher, over whose eyes we were able to pull the wool and trick into printing our work not once, but twice now!

I'd also like to give an enormous thanks to ass-cracks, side-boob, bad parents, jorts, tube tops, cross-dressers, drunks, drugs, muffin-tops, biscuit-bottoms, rednecks, tie-dye, the color-blind, pajamas, pimps, Goths, emos, sluts, states' inability to regulate shit on cars, bad hair, bad tattoos, costume lovers, and every other person out there who loves to express themselves in public. But most importantly, we want to thank our wonderful fantastic amazing magnificent dedicated fans who love to take pictures of the aforementioned people and send them in to us! We honestly could not do any of this without you and we love you all.

Just for the record it currently stands:

Adam, Luke, & Andrew–2 books published

Brandon Evans–0 books published

DISCLAIMER

We are in no way affiliated or associated with Walmart. We also personally have nothing against Walmart. We, along with most of America, shop at Walmart for nearly everything we need. This book and our website are simply satirical social commentary about the extraordinary sights found at America's favorite store. Walmart is Americana, baby!

All photographs and stories have been submitted by the users of www.PeopleofWalmart.com, the rights to which have been granted to ALA Design, LLC. Since we do not take the photographs ourselves, and many are taken with cell phone cameras, some of the pictures are not of the highest quality and may appear blurry and/or out of focus. So don't look at a picture and think you are losing your sight; it's just somebody's hand shaking excitedly as they run down the aisle with their camera phone.

WARNING: Some of the pictures and stories contained in this book are very graphic. We are not responsible if after reading a story or looking at a picture you have the sudden urge to vomit, stab yourself in the eye, stab a nearby coworker or friend, jump out a window, drink bleach, bathe in bleach, clean your eyes with bleach, quit your job and spend the rest of your life in a secluded cave, cut off a limb, become aroused (Really? That's sick!), rally people for a book burning, divorce your partner, skydive without a parachute, join the Taliban, or sell all your assets and give the money to us (actually, that last one is fine). So pretty much, continue reading at your own risk.

INTRODUCTION

To understand how we got the idea for People of Walmart, think back to your last trip to Wally World. Focus on everything you saw from the time you got out of your car in the parking lot, to picking up your supplies or groceries, to checking out and leaving. That car you saw with all the action figures glued to it–that's how we got the idea. That lady breast-feeding her kid who actually turned out to be a man breast-feeding someone else's kid–that is what inspired us. That 400-pound lady you saw but couldn't determine whether she had less teeth or clothes–she was our muse.

It's been more than three years now and we still have to say, "Holy Shit! We can't believe we are still around." The reason we are still kickin' is because of you guys. When we first started we had a simple blog with some funny pictures, but your insatiable appetite for the bizarre just couldn't be subdued, and you needed even more sick and twisted content to feed that hunger. So we listened, and we brought you stories and videos and our overflowing hate mail.

Soon your lust for laughter was so great that it could no longer be satisfied by our tiny little…website? Ya we'll go with website there. So you pushed us to give you what you wanted. We created the Three Ring Blog network with more than 25 different humor blogs to fulfill almost everyone's needs. You like chicks with nice butts? GirlsinYogaPants.com. Wanna see bubba's redneck ass fix something? WhiteTrashRepairs.com. Stupid drunk people? LateNightMistakes.com has you covered. You want some funny cats? Look somewhere else, because we don't like cats. Let's just say for the most part, we have whatever you need to get through your shitty day.

Over the years, and with all of our different websites, you would think our senses would have dulled to the crazy, gross, and nasty, but I'm still amazed by the amount of pictures, videos, and stories that you guys send in that still leave our jaws hanging on the ground. It really is because of all of you that we have grown into what we are now. So keep visiting the site, keep sending in great material, and we'll continue to keep you smiling. In the past three years there have been plenty of funny sites that have popped up and just as quickly faded away, but it's because of you guys that we've stuck around to keep entertaining the world. We like to think of ourselves like a nice pair of cutoff jorts—scary to look at, but never really go out of style. Actually scratch that, jorts were never really in style, but we still encourage others to wear them so you guys can take their picture.

So, there you have it. That, my friends, is how three assholes came up with PeopleofWalmart.com and how it blossomed into the beautiful flower it is today. Love it or hate it, our site is a reflection of our glorious nation and everyone's favorite place to shop. So either get on board or change your clothes, because one way or another you are a part of People of Walmart!

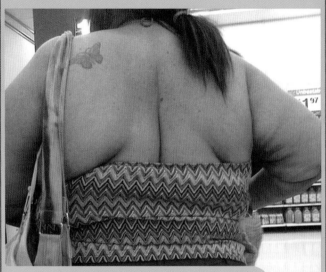

Wow, kinda impressive to have a back ass and back titties all in one! Some guys might call that one-stop shopping. I might call the ambulance to come pick me up after I set my eyes on fire.

AFTER A FEW BEERS

Wait a minute. I feel so violated. You've been lying to me this whole time!...You aren't a natural blond!

I guess even in the furry costume dress-up sex world there are the ones who no one wants to sleep with.

Pssssttttt, I don't want to be a dick, but can I suggest that just maybe you're not helping yourself by dressing like a marshmallow Peep?

Finally! I'm sick of seeing all those guys in spandex suits. Leave it to Charlie from *It's Always Sunny in Philadelphia* and the Green Men in Vancouver who go to the Canucks games. The rest of you—well I hope you run into this guy with the mallet.

Awww, I love those wacky wavy arm guys outside of businesses, but I'm sad that the economy is such crap that it's easier and cheaper to hire someone than it is to just buy one of those things.

SLEEPING BEAUTY

My wife and I go to Walmart every now and again to buy groceries (one of those huge Walmarts opened up near us!). We went in through the front door and tried to get a shopping cart from the cart line and noticed that the carts had a few large black garbage bags on top of them and what looked like a scarecrow lying on top. This was the first week of November, so I was thinking that some of the Halloween decorations were still up. I walked up to take a look, and sure enough, there was an old homeless man sleeping on top of the shopping carts with his bags right up there next to him…inside the Walmart.

FIND THE DIFFERENCES!

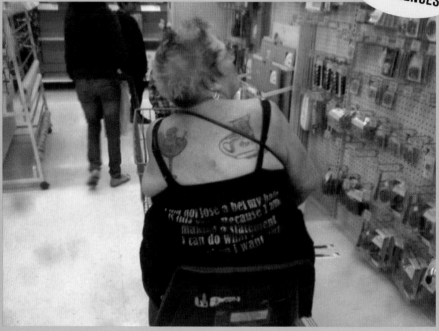

Hey parents, you know how you keep telling yourself that your punker kid is just going through a phase and will eventually grow out of it?...Yeah, keep telling yourself that.

CALIFORNIA

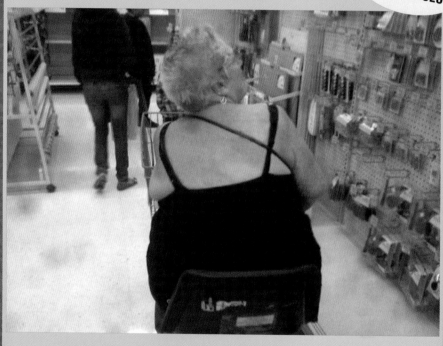

FIND THE
DIFFERENCES!

CALIFORNIA

THE LEGEND RETURNS

Our Hall of Famer, Magic School Bus Lady, is strutting her stuff once again, showing us why she is a legend and also how those ladies who attend the Kentucky Derby could take a few lessons from her…

Awesome! I swear those two dogs are a drummer away from starting the new ZZ Top, and I'm all for it.

SKULLF*CKER

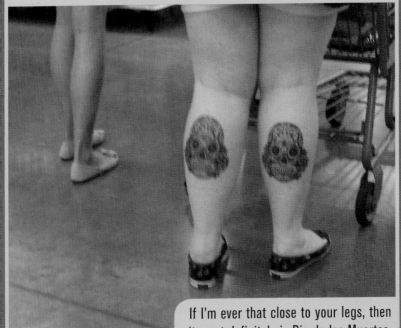

If I'm ever that close to your legs, then it most definitely is Dia de los Muertos.

BLOW MY WHISTLE, BITCH

They are either George Clinton groupies or something you sneak out on when you wake up next to them after a rave where you thought that ecstasy was a good idea.

THE SLING SHOT

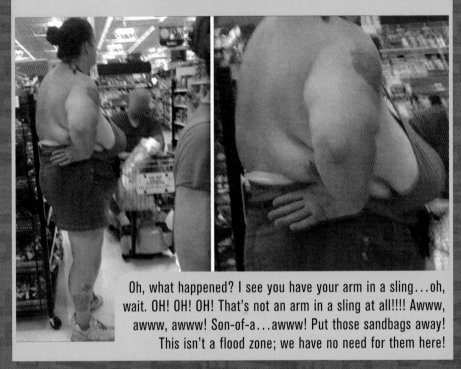

Oh, what happened? I see you have your arm in a sling...oh, wait. OH! OH! OH! That's not an arm in a sling at all!!!! Awww, awww, awww! Son-of-a...awww! Put those sandbags away! This isn't a flood zone; we have no need for them here!

FRESH-SQUEEZED LEMONADE

The other day, my wife, daughter, and I headed to Walmart to buy some groceries. We decided to split up and each find the needed items. I pushed the cart back to the refrigerated section to pick up eggs. Standing in the corner between the refrigerated cases, I saw a little kid standing there with his pants down to his ankles and his mom in front of him holding a McDonald's cup. She was allowing him to pee in this cup instead of taking him to the bathroom. I was a bit disgusted but decided to ignore it.

A moment later, the mom and kid had disappeared. I got what I needed, plus a few more impulse purchases, and happened to walk right by where the kid had been taking a leak into the cup just a few minutes before. There, sitting on the edge of the refrigerated case, was the McDonald's cup, full of pee, with the lid on it and a straw sticking out. I walked away, still trying to ignore all of this. A few seconds later, I heard an "ewww!" I turned and looked back and saw that some kid, about four or five, had picked up the drink and sipped from it, spitting the pee everywhere.

LIKE A LOLLIPOP

OH GOD! Some unfortunate kid is gonna wind up with those toys! Seriously, what is wrong with you? While you're answering that, I'm gonna go sterilize everything in my house that I ever bought.

Either this guy is drunk and getting arrested, or he pissed someone off and is about to be put into the Figure Four Leg Lock! Please, please, please, be the latter!

SKUNK'D

Ever drive past a dead animal on the road, then on your way back notice it's gone and wonder who picked it up and what they did with it?...Wonder no more.

BOTTOM HEAVY

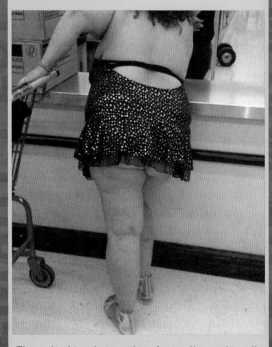

The only thing better than free rolls are big ol' bottom biscuits! Granted, both will probably leave you sick for days, but they're free, right?

GOING SKIING

I tried really, really, really hard to think of something other than her negotiating prices for going skiing on these two, but I just couldn't. I sincerely apologize for putting that in your head. For those of you who don't know what that means, just do yourself a favor and be thankful and don't Google it. For those of you who do, again, I'm really sorry.

CONSPIRACY TO MURDER

I'm an electronics associate, and I was covering for someone in the sporting goods section. Not five minutes after I got there, a woman called to ask about our CO_2 tanks for paintball guns. She asked about the toxicity of the gas. She then asked if I thought that said toxicity would kill a rabbit. I was a little startled by the question, but I managed to keep my hands clean of bunny murder by stating, "In no way could I advocate or endorse such an action on behalf of Walmart…but on a scientific basis, yeah."

This peach of a human being proceeded to describe how she bought a rabbit that was apparently diseased and was trying to kill it in a humane fashion because it was so tough to strangle the critters, and it took, like, six or seven knocks upside a tree to snap their necks. To which I could only reply, "…Yeah, they're really promiscuous, so I'd imagine they're not too eager to go to rabbit hell." She then asked about our propane canisters and mused about creating her own little gas chamber with a five-gallon paint bucket. I know I said that "Ma'am, I cannot advocate or endorse…" thing at least three times. The same woman called back five minutes later asking about the prices of our large insulated coolers. It didn't hit me until a couple minutes later that I had just signed the death warrant of some poor sick rabbit.

RIDING BAREBACK

Rodeo Girl—saving horses by riding cowboys since 1926.

Where's Gary?...Actually, on second thought, I don't think I wanna know.

Hey, watch out, lady! One speed bump and those hood ornaments of yours will be out for the world to see.

Did you just double up a ponytail with an epic rat tail that you started growing in the fifth grade? You have literally blown my mind, and now I won't be able to sleep for weeks thinking about everything that went into this hair decision.

BUDDY THE ELF

Fun Fact*: Apparently Buddy the Elf was supposed to be played by Chris Farley...in a Walmart.
*Editor's Note: We cannot confirm any shred of validity about this fact, making it, therefore, not really a fact at all.

I'll pay for my candy, thanks...

THE INTERESTING PURCHASE

I had to stop in Walmart for a few things for my mother. I was in line behind a young looking boy, and I couldn't tell what he was holding. He put his items on the belt, and it turned out to be three things: Vaseline, Ball Park Bun Size Franks, and Trojan condoms. The cashier looked at him and asked him how old he was. When he replied with eighteen, she asked to see his ID. Needless to say, he got angry and handed the cashier his ID. While she was checking it, I couldn't hold my laughter in anymore. He turned around and gave me the death stare. That just made me laugh even more, and soon everyone in line was laughing. The boy stalked off, with a red face and his lonely fun.

SANTA'S LITTLE HELPER

I'm just gonna go ahead and say that Mrs. Claus may want to start screening Santa's little helpers more closely.

MY LITTLE PONY

I wasn't aware they were making a live-action version of *My Little Pony*.

I have to say, that shirt really brings out the color of your testicles...

PROFESSOR GOOFBALL

Thank God that there are still mad scientists out there! I was really starting to get concerned that they were all being wiped out by the likes of Bugs Bunny, Scooby Doo, and town villagers.

KANSAS

BIG COCK COUNTRY!

Hmm, I always thought Kansas was the Sunflower State, but you are doing a hell of a job convincing me otherwise.

LATE NIGHT MISTAKE

I've been pretty wasted, but fortunately I've missed this level of drunk. However, you would feel right at home with the rest of the people over at LateNightMistakes.com.

TWO DICKS IN LINE

My wife and I had traveled for a wedding and had about an hour to kill before it started. We decided to swing by Walmart to pick up some stuff. We grabbed our stuff and went to the express line. The lady in front of us had just a few things, but the last thing didn't have a tag. I wasn't in a hurry, so it wasn't a big deal. One of the employees went to go check the price.

About thirty seconds into us standing there with a very apologetic cashier, this guy walked up with nothing in his hands. He stepped right between me and the lady who had been checking out, which was a space of two and a half feet. I looked at him, and he turned toward me, asking if I was in line. I said yes, and he looked confused. My wife replied, "We aren't just standing here for the hell of it; we are in line." He apologized and stood behind me. The clerk told him it would be a few moments, as they were waiting for a price check. He was shuffling back and forth, obviously agitated. He turned to me about twenty seconds later and asked why she was taking so long. I then realized that he was under the impression that I was another employee, which is understandable because I was dressed in black slacks, a tan button-up shirt, and sunglasses, and my wife was wearing a dress. I had about lost my patience and turned to him, replying, "I don't know. I don't fucking work here; why don't you back the fuck up?" He then gave me a look like I was the rudest person in the store. We left, with the jackass still staring at us as we walked out.

WELCOME TO OAKLAND, BITCH!

Hey, remember when the Oakland Raiders were good?
Those were good times…Yeah, so here is Cliff Branch.

CLIFF BRANCH
OF THE
OAKLAND RAIDERS
AUTOGRAPHS

15 YRS NFL
4 TIME ALL PRO
4 TIME ALL PRO BOWL
SUPER BOWL CHAMPIONS
XI, XV, XVIII

FIVE TAILS ARE BETTER THAN ONE

My dad always told me if you're gonna do something, either go big or go home. Unfortunately, this guy decided not to do us all a favor and go home.

ACID-WASHED

Well, that's what will happen when you let all that fromunda cheese rot and deteriorate your jeans.

THE DOUBLE BARREL

It's just like a double-barreled shotgun: big, loud, intimidating, and should never be out in public!

HEF'S MAIN SQUEEZE

They are just letting anyone into the Playboy Club nowadays, huh? Remind me to skip the issue that you're Playmate of the Month in.

UNKNOWN

NO CHILDREN, JUST DONKEYS

There is always one jackass in the parking lot who I want to donkey punch...Enough donkey puns for you? No? What if he was also smuggling drugs and I was able to throw in 'mule'? Would that do it for you? Still no? Damn, you people are hard to please!

I WILL NOT EAT CAT POOP!

I was working at Walmart in the customer service line when a lady slapped her return on the counter. The item was triple-bagged; I had to open all three to find out what she was returning. It was the worst thing I have ever smelled in my entire life and made me want to barf. The lady claimed that it was cat food, which happened to be in the shape of cat poop. That's right. The lady was attempting to return her cat's crap for a new can of cat food! Come on!

HO! HO! HO!

It's a People of Walmart photo within a People of Walmart photo! Once you recover from having your mind blown, I'm sure you can appreciate a back shot of our favorite holiday man! And hey, knock off the giggling at the "Ho's" being on his ass...seriously, guys, sometimes I don't know what to do with you all.

Everyday **Low Price**
$**8**^88

RANDOM CREEPY GUY

Once you get past French Fried Potaters here and the unavoidable booty in your face, is anyone else weirded out by the creep in the background popping his head over for a looky-loo? Seriously, those guys always give me the jeepers. Check 'em out over at RandomCreepyGuy.com and see if you can stand looking at them without that chill in your spine.

Wouldn't it be great if camo worked everywhere so you didn't have to see people wear it? Plus, I'm not a parent, but I would venture to guess that most little girls would rather play Barbie than learn how to field dress a dead deer.

RIPPED UP

WHO WEARS IT BETTER?

One of my favorite features is our "Who Wears It Better?" competition. I think this will be our "Hulk's Slam Piece" edition. So which ripper do you like: Pretty in Pink or the Dream Catcher?

JELLY BELLY

My initial guess is he is lecturing her about the *Book of Awesomeness*. It has three chapters. Chapter 1: Mullets. Chapter 2: Camo. Chapter 3: Exposure.

OHIO

Whatever you're ordering, I think it's safe to say they can hold the buns because you have just shown us all that you have enough already. McDonald's in Walmart is like a sweet, sweet marriage for us here at PoWM, but also over at FreaksofFastFood.com!

Everyone is always saying Tupac is alive somewhere, but I think we at PoWM have just started our own conspiracy theory for the Notorious B.I.G.

WHO ARE YOU CALLING A "LAZY ASS"?

Two years ago, while I was pregnant with my twin boys, my husband and I had to stop at the store to pick up a few things after one of my OB appointments (unfortunately, the only store on our way home was Walmart). I was about seven-and-a-half months pregnant at the time. While we were in the checkout line, I was starting to feel a bit dizzy, so I told my husband I was going to sit on one of the benches to wait for him. So I waddled my extremely pregnant behind to the closest bench and sat down. An older gentleman comes over and sits next to me. We start chatting, and all is fine. Then this ENORMOUS older gentleman comes over and FORCES his fat ass onto the bench. There wasn't enough room for the three of us. He looks at me and tells ME to "get my lazy fucking ass up" so he can sit down. I look at him with an "are you serious???" expression, and he tells me "you shouldn't have gotten your stupid teenage whore self knocked up." My husband was walking by at this time (and no, neither of us were teenagers; I was 23…I just look really young). My hubby EXPLODES on him, screaming how if he actually walked through Walmart instead of using a scooter, he wouldn't have to tell a pregnant woman to get off the bench.

SEWIN' IT SHUT

Just in case you didn't already know from learning the alphabet, nothing comes between *A* and *B*.

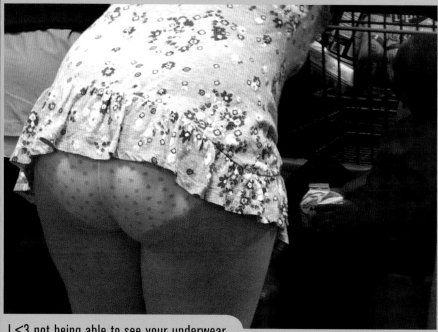

I <3 not being able to see your underwear.

HOW THE GRINCH STOLE DALMATIANS

If they ever make a movie where the Grinch also wants to steal 101 dalmatians, I think we've found our lead villain.

PENNY ON THE FLOOR

It's "penny for your thoughts," not "I'm gonna pay in pennies to piss off the cashier and hold this long-ass line up for twenty-five minutes."

THE DRIVE-BY

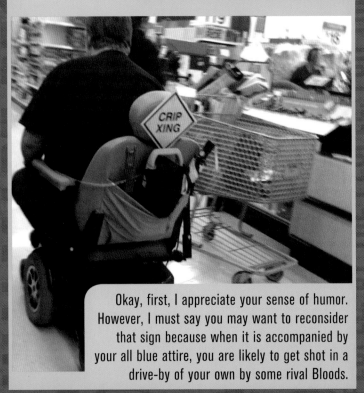

Okay, first, I appreciate your sense of humor. However, I must say you may want to reconsider that sign because when it is accompanied by your all blue attire, you are likely to get shot in a drive-by of your own by some rival Bloods.

♫ Hey, hey, we're the Monkees, and people say we monkey around ♫ —No. People don't say that anymore. They say, "Get that filthy little evil thing out of here before it takes out my kid's cornea."

HIT AND RUN

I used to be a stockman at Walmart, and one thing that occurred on a regular basis was people driving their cars…directly at me, either by accident or on purpose. Anyway, one specific "accident" that really stands out for me was a few months before I left the job. I was finishing up some restocking when I heard an argument going on at the front desk. This guy–let's call him redneck cliché, or RNC–was bitching because the lady at the front desk wouldn't return a four-year-old boob tube at the price of a 32" plasma. RNC kept saying he bought this "plasma TV" yesterday. Anyway, to make a four-hour story short, he left pissed off. A few minutes later, I go out to get carts, and all of a sudden I hear a loud truck heading toward me. I turn around just in time to get hit by RNC. I roll over his truck and land on my face, and when I look up, I see him slow down to yell "Fuck you Walmart!!! I'll never shop here again." A week later, I saw RNC in the electronics department looking for a new TV.

THE ADULT MUNCHKIN

Listen, Bub, you no longer represent the Lollipop Guild, so grow up, get out of Munchkin Land mode, and move on!

LADIES AND GENTLEMEN, MR. CONWAY TWITTY FAN

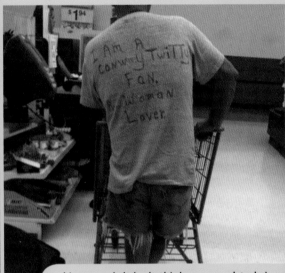

Listen, pal, I don't think you need to bring your Craigslist post with you everywhere you go. My best advice would be to come off a little more subtle. Maybe park outside of a tractor pull with a six-pack of Budweiser tall boys, and you'll find the right one.

Where are all my Hulkamaniacs at?...Good, now that I've found you all, I can tell you that his time is over and you can knock it off immediately.

THE PATRIOTIC PATOOT

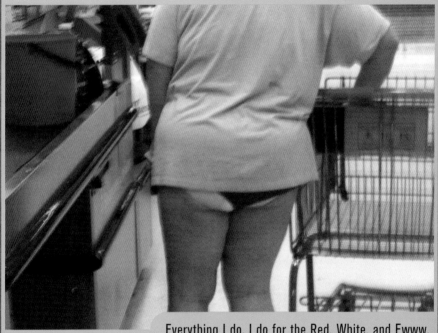

Everything I do, I do for the Red, White, and Ewww.

LITTLE SLICE OF HEAVEN

Sweet sassy molassy! If that thing
is your heaven, what is your hell?

SOME PEOPLE SAY CUCUMBERS TASTE BETTER PICKLED

Though this story isn't about horrors from the restrooms or devil children, it still made me sick. Like most of you, I only venture to my local Walmart when it's the only viable option. I can't remember what I needed at the time, but I rounded an aisle in the grocery department that had the fewest people in it, you know, to speed up my journey. As I came to the end of the aisle, I stayed clear of the two ladies loitering. For whatever reason, I looked up. That's when I saw one lady pull a huge jar of pickles off the shelf, open it up, cram her nasty fingers into the jar, and pull out a pickle. She took a bite out of it, chewed it with a quizzical expression, PUT THE REST OF THE PICKLE BACK IN THE JAR, closed it up, and put it back on the shelf. All she said to her friend was "nah," and they slowly sauntered away. I've always thought that safety seals were to help stop intentional poisonings, but since that occasion, I check all of my safety seals with the utmost seriousness.

THE WALMART NINJA

I see Tum Tum from *3 Ninjas* grew up and managed to find himself a lady friend. Completely unexpected, but good for him!

TORPEDOES

Holy schnikes, is it cold out here! Forget glass, those torpedoes could cut through a bank safe!

WASHINGTON

Ahh yes, I see you've found the rare miniature albino whale that likes to hide in the undercarriage of women's asses! Typically they are very hard to find, due to their hosts having the common sense not to wear see-through white, but every now and then we get a rare glimpse at this creature.

I'm sure you two are the cutest couple at the county fair!

USED UNDIES

My boyfriend and I were walking around Walmart after eating a hearty dinner at Old Country Buffet (classy, I know). He had to take a dump, so he ran into the bathroom. When he was finished and went to wipe, he reached into the toilet paper dispenser to grab some TP and instead pulled out someone else's shit-covered blue Fruit of the Loom underwear. Apparently, after shitting your pants, it's more convenient to throw the underwear in the toilet paper dispenser than in the garbage can.

...AND TWINS!

How adorable is it when old twins dress alike? It's nice to see solidarity in their complete loneliness for male companionship.

SWEATER PUPPIES

Wow! Cute sweaters...How 'bout we try to man the f*ck up for a few minutes?

UNKNOWN

Monkeys are only cool when they are (1) picking bugs off each other and eating them, (2) flinging poop, and (3) furiously masturbating. But I don't want to see any of that while I'm shopping.

FIGHTING LOW PRICES

Superwoman and Mighty Mouse love shopping at Walmart because, oddly enough, they don't have to get out of costume to blend in.

BUNNY LOVE

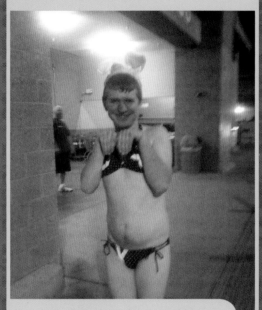

Hey there, little fuzzy bunny wabbit,
why don't you hop hop hop into traffic?

OVER/UNDERALLS

That's quite a fashion statement. Sure, it says "these belong to a much shorter painter," but that's still quite a statement.

THONG SONG

A few years ago, I worked at Walmart at the returns desk. As everyone knows, good old Walmart takes back everything. I had gone on my break when this particular return happened. A man approached the returns desk with about ten pairs of women's thong underpants. My coworker was unfortunate enough to help him out. It is customary to ask why you are returning the product and what is wrong with it. The man's response: "My wife bought these underwear, and they all ride up her ass, so she asked me to return them for her." The man's wife had worn every pair before coming to this conclusion.

With everyone's obsession with using Twitter these days, I thought I would have seen my fill of ridiculous Tweets over at DumbTweets.com, but I have to say, this is past obsession and into seeing-a-shrink level.

Okay, now I've heard of vanity plates, but never vanity mirrors on a car! But sometimes you got to make due, I suppose. To see more crazy-ass fixes next time you get on your laptop (which is probably just a desktop with an extension cord), make sure you check out WhiteTrashRepairs.com.

Dear Captain Jackass, nobody finds grown men who dress up amusing. It's sad and weird.

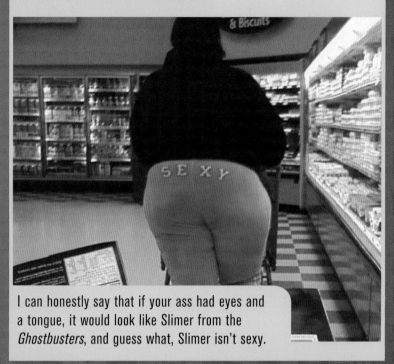

YOU KNOW I'M SEXY

I can honestly say that if your ass had eyes and a tongue, it would look like Slimer from the *Ghostbusters*, and guess what, Slimer isn't sexy.

FEMININE ITCHING

My husband and I were at Walmart filling a prescription for my dog (yes, I know, weird). There are always a lot of "characters" at my particular Walmart, and it's usually a good laugh. As we were walking toward the pharmacy, we saw this short, kind of chubby chick. She was wearing a tight (very tight) red dress that you could almost see her butt cheeks in, complete with fishnet stockings and 5-inch stilettos. My husband and I laughed, made our usual comment about hookers, and walked away. We wandered around for a bit until my pup's prescription was filled. We got back up to the pharmacy, and in front of us is Ms. Hooker herself. She was at the consultation window and was asking the pharmacist about over-the-counter medication for "feminine itching." The pharmacist asked her what she had tried, and she started listing items. The pharmacist, who was an older man, blushed and told her to go to the doctor. She stormed off, saying she couldn't go to the doctor and complaining about how bothersome her little problem was. My husband and I struggled to hold back the laughter until she was gone, at which point everyone around us started cracking up.

THE MOUNTAINEER

Now personally, I like to live indoors, so all of this…whatever this is…seems ridiculous to me. However, I do have to say I'm kinda impressed at the handmade cart that may or may not also double as a baby stroller/deer carcass carrier.

FOXY LADY

I see Wile E. Coyote has finally given up chasing the Road Runner and decided to retire somewhere on the outskirts of where I assume *Deliverance* was filmed. Nice job finding jorts with a tail hole, by the way.

Hahaha! Whose idea was it to put a referee shirt on a zebra? Classic! It hurts my eyes, but classic!

THE CHRISTMAS ONESIE

Quick, somebody go grab that ball that fell off the Christmas tree before someone steps on it...or it steps on someone.

Tell 'em, brother! The day you can't wear those boots in public is the day I'm leavin' Amurrrica for good!

2PAC BACK

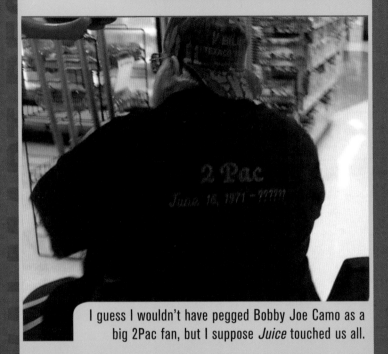

2 Pac
June 16, 1971 - ??????

I guess I wouldn't have pegged Bobby Joe Camo as a big 2Pac fan, but I suppose *Juice* touched us all.

ONE HELL OF AN ENTRANCE

This happened while I worked at a local Walmart a few years back as an inventory control specialist (I unloaded the truck and put groceries on the shelves–fancy name for a shitty job). It was a busy summer day, about three in the afternoon, the shoppers out in droves, the sun shining, and the sound of squealing metal and shattering glass filling the air. This last part seemed a bit out of the ordinary, so my coworker and I dropped what we were doing and wandered up front to see what had happened. In the west entrance of the store, a large red truck had managed to miss the concrete poles outside the entry but had plowed into a shopping cart filled with groceries and one of the sliding glass doors, including all the connecting framework into the inside wall. The shopper who the cart belonged to had escaped unharmed, but we were too busy watching the driver to really notice. He was maybe ninety years old and was trying to walk into the store like nothing had happened, like he was just there to shop and hadn't destroyed one of our entrances (easily the most destructive customer I saw in my two years at that store).

The next day in the back, someone had added a truck sticker to the map we mark the locations of accidents on. That sticker was still there when I left, more than a year later. Always had a bit of a laugh whenever walking past.

KNOW YOUR ANIME

My parents never let me leave the house looking like this, but then again my parents weren't Japanese Anime characters.

RUBBER DUCKY, YOU'RE THE ONE

Rubber Baby Buggy Bumpers. Rubber Baby Buggy Bumpers. Rubber Baby Buggy Bumpers…Hmm, it's much easier to say than look at. Grow up, baby ducky!

I see we found Burger King's personal shaman...or we found that lady who lives in the creepy house where the grass hasn't been cut in 14 years.

BLAST FROM THE PAST

Excuse me, miss, the 2 Live Crew music video taping is actually back over there in 1991.

VIRGINIA

NAMING CONTEST: LET'S PLAY DRESS UP!

Okay, everyone, if you've followed us on the website, then you've seen this legend many times before. Unfortunately, unlike the rest of our Hall of Famers, this sexy guy doesn't have a name yet. So do us a favor and send your ideas to info@peopleofwalmart.com because this is your chance to make history!

This guy's name should be:_____

Your name:_____

Location:_____

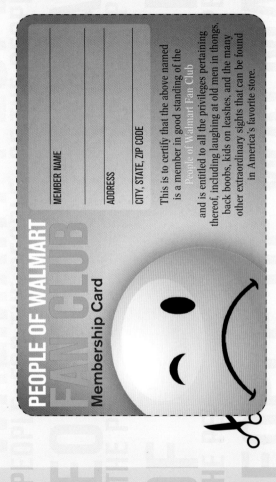

If this guy isn't the poster child for my emotions every time I walk into Walmart and it's asses-to-elbows, then I don't know who the hell is.

MARTY POPPINS

So who is gonna step up and let Mary Poppins here watch their kids? Really? No takers? What if he shaved his mustache? Still no? I'm disappointed in all of you.

♫ Slow ride, take it easy. Slow ride, take it easy. ♫ Well said, Foghat. Ignoring your kid while she tries to water ski behind you is probably not what they had in mind, but I think it fits.

FEAR WHITEY

As I was walking toward the checkout at Walmart, I heard the shrill shriek of a crying four- to six-year-old boy. I looked around to see where his parents were and didn't notice anyone. I stared at the kid debating whether I should get an employee to help out, when out of the blue came his mom. She told him, "See! People are staring and laughing at you. You better stop crying, or the 'white' people are going to tell on you!" I didn't know what was weirder, that she told her very young son to fear white people or that she has no problem pointing out that society laughs at his misery. I'm going to go with the racism.

OOPS, I TOOK A POOP

I don't think anal tie-dye is going to catch on anytime soon.

SHAKE YOUR MONEY-MAKER

Thanks for mooning us. And by "mooning," I don't mean showing us your ass, I mean showing us your thighs, which look like the craters of the moon. No wonder NASA stopped the space program.

I don't think John's words apply to *SpongeBob SquarePants*. He is made of sponge, not flesh.

DOIN' IT DOGGY STYLE

"I'll teach you to leave me in the hot car sweating my damn nuts off while you shop! I hope you plan on buying some paper towels and stain remover sucker!"

THE BANDANA BANDIT

I see the apple doesn't fall far from the tree. Unfortunately, that tree has about as much going for it as Charlie Brown's Christmas tree.

THE PERFECT MATCH

FIND THE DIFFERENCES!

What did you two write on your Match.com profiles? "Looking for someone who also enjoys looking like they fell victim to a prank while passed out drunk"?

FIND THE DIFFERENCES!

THE GREATEST MULLET OF OUR TIME

Oh, sweet baby Jesus! The mullet, the snow, the look of despair! I only wish Bob Ross was still alive, because I would commission him to paint this portrait for me to hang in my living room!

IDAHO

Well, fortunately for us, we can now see you coming from the next aisle over, so we can avoid you just like the rest of society already has.

PICTURE ME NAKED

I worked overnight at a small Walmart Supercenter several years ago. For some reason, at this particular store, we had all kinds of crazy things happen! From people having diarrhea leakage on the sales floor to one of my fellow associates catching a couple having full-on sexual intercourse up against the back wall in the far corner of the garden center during closing time. But my favorite story of all was the man who would come in our store at night before closing time and leave a Polaroid picture of his erect penis on the floor of the women's dressing room! This happened more than once, if I remember correctly. I am not certain if they ever caught the guy because I believe he knew to do this at night when there was no one watching the dressing rooms. The doors on the dressing rooms were kept locked, of course, but all he had to do was slide the picture underneath. I still laugh to this day when I think of that story, wondering if that guy actually thought he was doing some kind of service to whomever would find his pictures!

Hey, it's Joyce Dewitt from the hit show *Three's Company*!...Go ahead and turn the page. It's my own book and I don't really give a damn either.

Listen, I wasn't gonna say anything, but now that you bring it up, you have been acting a bit Kunt-ish.

Kid, I too would worry that I'd grow up and have nothing better to do than dress up like a zombie. Fortunately, you will most likely have friends, family, responsibilities, and a life to help keep you occupied enough that you won't have to do stupid crap like this.

ICE YOUR OWN CAKE

I'm sick of places implementing these "do-it-yourself" ploys. The last thing I need is to come into a store and ice my own cake while a nipple hair from Bubba walking around shirtless floats into my "Happy Retirement" icing design!

SHE CALLED FIVES

Are you really playing security guard over a parking spot? Seriously? I know Americans in general are lazy as hell, but to go out of your way to further your own laziness and avoid walking seems a tad stupid. This isn't a seat in high school that you can call fives on, it's the real world, jackass.

PEE PANTS

I was at a Super Walmart waiting to return something, and I smelled something bad; it was like being on the subway. I thought maybe it was someone in line, but they seemed to be smelling it too. I noticed this woman sitting on the floor in front of the pop machine drinking a bottle of water with a wild and crazy daze on her face. I turned my head; when I looked back, she wasn't there, but there was a huge puddle. I was wondering if she spilled her bottle of water, but the smell was even worse now. A couple of minutes later, a Walmart employee came by with a mop and bucket, mumbling and swearing under his breath—the crazy lady peed on the floor through her pants!

ASK ME ABOUT MY WIENERS

.........sorry I passed out from the sudden rush of wiener jokes that flew to my brain!

DIAPER DANDY

Maybe I should commend you for your Black Friday commitment. Or maybe I should point out that not only is that flippin' ludicrous, but you're also a moron who can't figure out that diapers go on the inside. At least be ridiculous correctly!

Twenty items or less really is an arbitrary number. Fight the power, lady! I'm sure you're not as rude and thoughtless as you appear...

GIRL IN YOGA PANTS

Her six-pack and my six-pack are completely different...our camel toe, however, is the same. Wait, what? Ignore that last part. For more hard bodies in yoga pants, check out GirlsinYogaPants.com or go to the gym and get caught looking like a pervert.

The Irish: getting drunk and ruining non-St. Patrick's Day holidays since the 1820s.

FANNY PACKED IN TIGHT

Let's see if you can spot one thing that is **NOT** wrong with this picture.

Toy Story 4: Andy is 42 and still lives with his mom.

FISHY SITUATION

One day in 2009, I went to Walmart to visit my boyfriend, who was working there. While I was waiting for him to go on break, a lady came in and was raising complete hell at the service desk because the fish she had for a week had all died. Once she figured out they weren't going to give her money back, she got angry and stomped off into the bathroom to flush the fish. The people at customer service thought she had left but, surprise, she hadn't. She went to the fish tanks, filled up her container, and caught her own fish. She almost made it out the door before security caught her.

Okay, now once you're done looking at the skunk, get ready...go on, get ready...are you ready?...I'm pretty sure there's a child in the bottom part of the cart.

WHO WEARS
IT BETTER?

OREGON

WHO WEARS IT BETTER?

Awww, it looks like we might have found ourselves a love match here. Now they can tell each other to f*ck off and save the rest of us from putting up with their crap.

BACK IT UP

I couldn't think of anything better than that mesh top
to compliment those short white sweatshorts. Sexy.

I don't even know why you are bothering to look at bikinis because I don't think you could look any sexier. If I were you, I'd be over in the jewelry section picking out bellybutton rings, if you really want to make it pop, ya know!

C IS FOR COOKIE

Om nom nom nom...Me want ruin your kids' hopes and dreams!

It's a scene like this that brings the wise words of Young Jeezy to my mind: "Drop the top, no bra, got the titties out." Truly inspirational stuff. Now if you'll excuse me, I have to go to the emergency room because my eyes seem to be bleeding for some reason.

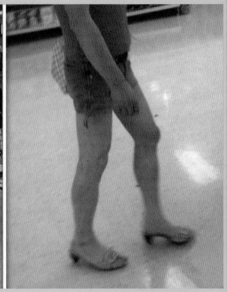

"Does something need to be licked? I heard there was something here that needed to be licked. Come on, what needs a good licking?"

PANTY RAID

The other morning I was running a register and an elderly lady came to me asking if I could give her change for a dollar. We're not supposed to give any sort of change out of our tills unless it's part of a transaction, but for a small amount, most of us break the rule and do it anyhow. I explained to her, as the person I was helping paid with a credit card, that I would if my till opened, but it didn't.

She moved on from register to register trying to get change, and the whole time, the other cashiers and I were trying to figure out what she had on her head. I had assumed it to be one of those satin hair wraps we see worn in the store a lot, but this seemed to have bits missing from it. We were speculating silently to ourselves as she finally got that change from someone's till, but it wasn't until she was leaving that one of the other cashiers figured out what it was on her head. "That woman's got panties on her head." I turned to look, because surely she had to be wrong. Who on earth would go out in a public store wearing panties on their head? Sure enough, though, for all the world to see, the old woman was wearing a pair of black silk panties on her head.

"O" NOT NECESSARY

Does anybody have any beanbags? I'm really in the mood to play some cornhole.

DRAG RACE

Well, obviously the front basket is full, so she can't ride E.T.-style, which doesn't leave her many other unsafe transportation options.

PIMP MY SCOOTER

$159

I'm sure this dude is still pickin' up mad hunnies in that ride, but if you're not gonna put 20-inch spinners on the thing, then why bother? Am I right, or am I right?

The irony here is overwhelming. I'm just going to sit back and let you soak it in.

TRASH

SUMMER GIRLS

Summertime means that we all get to witness more gems like this one.

"Well, I was born without the top of my skull, and I guess a little bit of my brains was showin', and it was grossin' everybody out, so my mom put this wig on me to cover it up, and then the bones grew together, and it got all infused and entwined. I mean, I don't mean to get all scientific with you…"

SNIFF, SNIFF

So my mom and I go into Walmart to cash a check since the banks were closed that day. We get in line at the service counter and wait our turn. We were waiting there for about three minutes when this guy came in and got in line behind us. We waited there for another couple minutes when I felt something breathing on my hair. THIS MAN WAS UP AGAINST ME SNIFFING MY HAIR!!! I turned around and asked him what he was doing, and he said–I kid you not–"I was just seeing if you were worth bringing home with me." Needless to say, my mom and I left that store and have not gone back since.

It's one thing to adopt a culture, and it's another thing to completely f*ck it up.

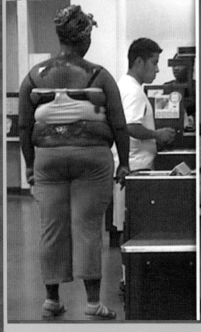

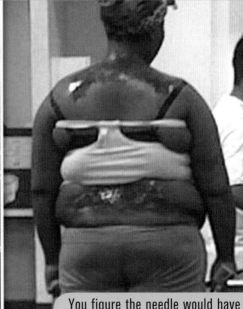

You figure the needle would have popped something, right?

Ummm, what the hell do you think you're doing? This is a Walmart aisle, not a scary movie where a bunch of pretty teenage girls' cars break down in the pouring rain.

ON A SESAME SEED BUN

No wonder the Hamburglar always gets caught! You are being so obvious!

I HIGHLY DOUBT THAT

Unfortunately, it looks like your mom was a ratf*cker.

Well, the good news is that we were able to crown our top mother from Mother's Day! Congratulations?

I'D HAMMER IN THE MORNING

When Walmart opened its first store years ago in my small hometown, it was an event that was much anticipated. My brother swore that he witnessed this exchange personally: A woman was attempting to purchase a package of Tampax that, for some reason, would not scan. The cashier therefore called for the manager, Mr. Strange (my brother swore that was his name, too) to do a price check–over the intercom, no less. "Mr. Strange, price check on Tampax. Mr. Strange, price check on Tampax." I can imagine the face of the customer at this point, but the best was yet to come. Believing that he had heard a request for a price check on TACKS, Mr. Strange approached the customer to ask, "Is that the kind you drive in with a hammer, or the kind you push in with your thumb?"

PLENTY UP TOP

♫ Ow, she's a brick (da-na-na-na) HOUSE. She's mighty mighty, just lettin' it all hang out. ♫

A+ for accessorizing with baby shoes! A++ for the balls! I was wondering about the baby's gender, and that's just an unexpected touch of class.

SCRUNCH TIME

WHO WEARS IT BETTER?

WHO WEARS IT BETTER?

Unlike people, scrunchies never get old... wait, I'm sorry, I'm getting word that scrunchies actually stop being cute at age 12. My bad for the misinformation earlier.

Hey! Hey! Hey, man, hold up. There's a f*ckin' jellyfish on your head! Stay still, I'll pee on it.

I guess when nobody else takes the throne, somebody has to step up to the plate.

"My boyfriend's segmented ponytail is so magical, it shrunk my clothes."

Are you trying to sneak that kid out of the store or something? Well, now that I think of it, if it's not your kid, then that's not a bad idea, I guess. I don't know, I don't steal kids anymore.

USED LUBE

I was once working the customer service desk when a woman in her mid-forties approached me with a small bag and placed it on the counter. She was a frightening sight, hair bleached one too many times and clothes mismatched and filled with holes. As she laid the bag on my counter, she leaned in and whispered, "I need to make a return." I replied, trying to remain as friendly as I could toward the end of my shift, "Well, you've come to the right place." I placed one hand in the bag as I asked, "Was the product defective?" to which the woman began vigorously nodding her head. She then proceeded to tell me that she had bought this personal lubricant a few days ago, and it had definitely not been to her satisfaction. "Ever since I used, this there has been burning and bleeding...down there. It even ate the polish off of my fingernails!" she explained as she thrust her fingers into my face.

At this point, everyone in line took a step back, and everyone behind the counter (all women old enough to be my mother) took a step toward me to see how their 19-year-old coworker would handle the situation. I apologized profusely to the woman while politely sliding the economy-sized bottle of hand sanitizer across the counter. "I would like to speak to your manager about this personally, so he will pull this off the shelf. Will you go get him, please?!" She was beginning to get agitated at this point. "Ma'am, he's not in the store at the moment, but I'll be SURE to pass along your story as soon as he comes back," I replied, laying her refunded money on the counter (I just couldn't bring myself to place it in her hand). She practically ran from the counter, and then the entire service desk area erupted with laughter. It has been three years, but to this day, if someone hands me a tied up bag, I ALWAYS ask what it is before sticking my hand in the bag, and I make sure I use hand sanitizer after every transaction.

SWAMP THING

Ladies and gentlemen, when we move into summer, the temperature rises and so does the unfortunate "Swamp Ass" epidemic. So be aware and try to stay dry!

I guess she was going for that "apple bottom" look.

SWEET TOOTH

I read an article recently that said hookers love cupcakes. That doesn't have anything to do with this photo, just something I thought you might find interesting.

How the hell did the White Witch of Narnia come through the wardrobe?

ALL THE WAY TURNT UP

FIND THE DIFFERENCES!

Sweet pair of Jordans, but I like the skirt better. Especially when you are dunking over me. It really helps for me to see that the balls are literally in my court.

FIND THE DIFFERENCES!

THE WALMART PLAYPEN

That is a great playpen! It's free, high enough that sketchy characters won't even notice an unwatched kid, plus there are a ton of diapers in case he needs to go. Throw him up there with a bag of Doritos and a two-liter of Mountain Dew, and you could take a nice long weekend without paying a babysitter.

You look like a human cupcake, which is sweet. Pun completely intended.

DIAPERLESS BABY

I had been out running and the lace on my shoe broke, so on my way home I decided to stop at Wally World and get a new one. Once I got to Walmart, I decided I'd just get a new pair of shoes. You can't argue with 15 bucks. I walked back to the shoe section, and a little boy maybe two years old was standing at the end of the row looking down. It looked like he didn't have pants on and only one shoe. I walked through a different row to avoid him, and as I came to the end, he was still standing there with his head down. He was looking at a diaper he had taken off and left on the ground about three feet away from him. The diaper was, of course, full. His dad poked his head past the corner and spotted him. The dad yelled his name and started walking down the row. As soon as the boy heard his father yell his name, he took off straight through the diaper and left tracks of baby shit along the floor behind him.

♫ Domo Arigato Mrs. Roboto, Domo (Domo), Domo (Domo). ♫

OH, COME ON! How hard could it possibly be to cover your ass?
The purpose of suspenders is to keep your pants up above your
waist, yet somehow you have managed to fail at that simple task,
while at the same time—just our luck—the backup safeguard of your
shirt has failed to stay down and protect us. Thanks, buddy!

Who thought it would be a good idea to cast the *No Country for Old Men* guy as the new Robin Hood?

HOT POTATO

Hey baby, your name must be Idaho because your ass looks like a big ol' spud, and I feel like playing hot potato!...Sorry, I'm not very good at pickup lines.

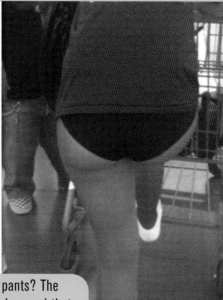

You know who wants everyone to wear pants? The Communists, that's who. Wrap your head around that.

THAT POOP AGAIN!

I work at Walmart, and about a week ago I came across some brown marks on the floor made by a cart's wheels and shoes. I followed it and found a PILE OF SHIT! Because my job description does not say that I have to pick up those brown beauties, I called for the janitor to come collect the offending nuggets. He looked as if he was going to throw up when he noticed the smell was seeping through the garbage bag. Who shits in the middle of a Walmart? I guess this isn't the first time we have found turds in the store. I had quite a few other coworkers tell me their poop-finding stories.

I was not aware that barbers were still using the salad bowl as a styling instrument, OR maybe she just happens to be a pee wee soccer player from 1992.

NO HITTER

How is it that I'm counting five different articles of clothing, and yet NONE of them fit? O for 5! Really? You aren't trying to get a hit off of C. C. Sabathia, you're putting on clothes!

Hey, Hulk Hogan, guys with a full head of hair look stupid with ponytails. Wanna take a guess how good it looks without half your hair?

PUT IT BACK

Do you REALLY think you are going to be needing those condoms there, playboy? Unless you plan on practicing for the "big game" with a toilet paper roll and some lunch meat, I recommend that you put them back on the shelf.

We would like to stress once again: "Please do not attempt to imitate anything you see in this book. These individuals are the exact opposite of trained professionals, and you will probably get hurt, be laughed at, and/or die."

STOP, THIEF!

The other day I locked my keys in the car while shopping at our local Walmart. I called home and proceeded to wait on the bench with the sweetest little old lady. We sat chatting, her waiting for her ride to pick her up and me waiting for my grandpa to come with the extra set of car keys. After sitting there talking for about ten minutes, a woman comes walking quickly out the doors with a woman in her twenties and a man around thirty following swiftly behind. The young woman quickly darted in front of the other woman, stopping her before she could get outside. She says, "My name is 'so-and-so' with Walmart security. Do you know why I am stopping you?" As she says "with Walmart security," she pulls her NAME TAG out of her pocket and flashes it like a badge. Not a security badge, not even a security name tag, just a regular old Walmart employee name tag. I could not help but giggle. Turns out the woman in question had her pockets full of makeup and Glade air freshener. After much arguing, and the woman trying to get away, they finally were able to get her into their office. I turn to the old lady, who was watching the whole scene with me, and say, "Well, that's not good." The old lady looks at me and says, "She should've taken a cane and hit the shit out of her. All that fuss over some spray freshener." I about fell off the bench laughing.

He was recently diagnosed with Pee Wee Herman Syndrome. Basically, your kids are distracted by him, and you have a sneaking suspicion that you shouldn't let them watch him, but for some reason you let them anyway.

MOHAWK VS. FROHAWK

I'm going to have to give the edge here to Shamus O'Toole because of the sweet Abe Lincoln chinstrap, but that's just me.

BLACK AND YELLOW

I feel like any minute now a big arm-bar is going to swing out with a Stop sign on it.

HOUND DOG

Before he died, did Elvis get a poodle pregnant? I don't know, but I'm not here to judge…Okay, I am, but still.

MOONS OVER MY HAMMY

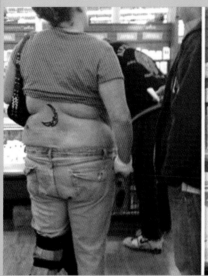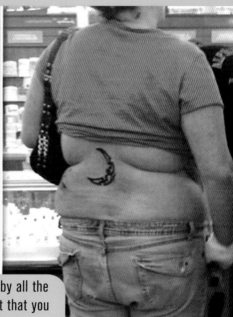

We landed on the moon! You can tell by all the rolling hills and craters...and the fact that you would want a spacesuit before touching down.

URINE TROUBLE

The only time I tried shopping for clothes at Walmart was in mid-summer in California, so I was wearing sandals. I took them off so I could try on a pair of shorts and realized that the dressing room carpet was soaking wet. Then I noticed the unmistakable smell of urine. I hustled out of there, and when I told the girl working the dressing room counter that someone had definitely peed in the dressing room, she just gave a "not again" sigh, pulled out a bucket of cleaning sprays stored under the counter, and trudged into the dressing room to get rid of the smell.

Oh damn, Santa is workin' it!

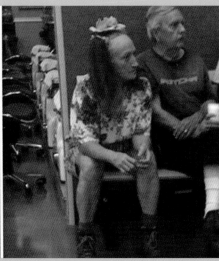

I DON'T WANNA GROW UP

Hey, Toys"R"Us kid, it's officially time to grow up.

I think that triangle is a scratch-n-sniff. Go on, try it.

♫ They're creepy and they're kooky, mysterious and spooky, they're all together ooky, the Addams Family. ♫

The Holiday Man and PoWM would like to wish everyone a Happy Easter and let you know that his van rides are still available.

NICK NOLTE'S SON

One day while working, I was on my way to use the facilities when I happened upon a man attempting to use a card in an ATM. He stopped me and told me he was having difficulty using it. Despite the obvious pin number written on the card and its poor condition, I answered his questions and directed him to speak to the clerks in the bank if he couldn't resolve the problem.

The next day I saw him standing in customer service speaking with one of the associates. I noticed then that he was obviously a drifter because he was dressed in the same clothes from the day before.

On the third day this gentleman wandered over to my department and proceeded to oogle over behind the bread wall. Then he poked his head behind the produce doors and wandered into the meat department. Everyone looked to me to go speak with him, so I did. He asked for some boxes, which I gave him. Then he started having a lengthy discussion with me. He was carrying a satchel, which he claimed held a story written about him and his father. He proceeded to push the issue about the story and how he needed the boxes to pack his belongings into because he was going home to his father in California. Then he told me I knew his father. The whole time I am trying to be polite, but I am trying to get back into the bakery behind the swinging doors. He then proceeds to tell me that I should know who his dad is and how he looks just like him. Then he tells me he is Nick Nolte's son. I tried to be impressed, but I know I failed. He then thanked me for his boxes and left. I was teased terribly by my coworkers and asked why I didn't get his autograph.

Oh that's so crazy! I just read an interesting article about how you all seem weird enough to get kicked out of a Harry Potter fan club meeting.

I would like to officially nominate those pants for worst color option EVER! Are you serious with that? "Hey, let's get skintight pants, make them in sizes where the word 'skintight' should be off-limits, and then produce them in a flesh color." You should be fired for that idea.

I've heard of junk in the trunk, but I wish you would pack it into an SUV instead of a Geo Metro.

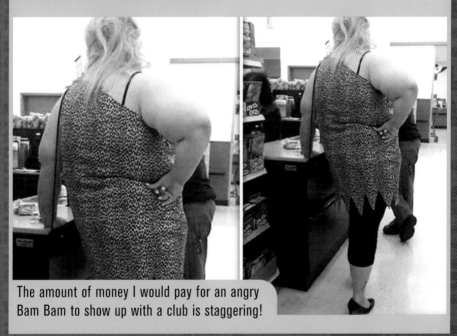

I CAN MAKE YOUR BEDROCK

The amount of money I would pay for an angry
Bam Bam to show up with a club is staggering!

FEEDING TIME

That's a full-on fully, man.

BUILT FORD TOUGH

Let me take a minute and introduce everyone to Rob Ford. Rob Ford is the mayor of Toronto (that's in Canada for all you non-hockey fans). I think it's now safe to assume that every person in the city of Toronto could be on PeopleofWalmart.com. If this is their mayor out in his jammies, then I have to believe every other Torontonian dresses as if they should be on our site! I'm sorry guys, blame your leader for this one.

We always joke around saying you can find everything at Walmart…even your wife.

UNKNOWN

OHIO

"As fans of PeopleofWalmart.com, we hosted our own People of Walmart party in Nashville, TN. We thought it would be a great idea to take pictures at Walmart... barely anyone seemed to think that there was anything wrong with what we were wearing."

CANDACE

FAN PHOTOS!

everyday Low Price $10

204

UNKNOWN

These girls walked around Walmart dressed like cows screaming in the meat section and filling up milk gallons.

JACK

FAN PHOTOS!

206

UNKNOWN

MANDI, CRYSTAL, AND RACHEL

FLORIDA

RACHEL

FAN PHOTOS!

Found the Wonka Bars in the chocolate aisle.

FAN PHOTOS!

Just a normal day at Walmart…

CALIFORNIA

Rump roast special, aisle 6.

UNKNOWN

FAN PHOTOS!

Family Christmas shopping

UNKNOWN

ABOUT THE AUTHORS

Adam Kipple, Andrew Kipple, and Luke Wherry all grew up in the same town of Harrison City, Pennsylvania, located just outside of Pittsburgh. Adam (28) is a web designer who graduated from the Art Institute of Pittsburgh and currently resides in Myrtle Beach, South Carolina, along with Luke (26), a graduate of the University of Pittsburgh, and Andrew (26), a graduate of Xavier University and Valparaiso University School of Law. The trio recently expanded their website properties into the humor blog network "Three Ring Blogs," which now houses more than 25 hilarious websites, and also opened their web design/marketing company in Myrtle Beach.